Kingfisher Young Discoverers

ENERGY
AND
POWER

ROSIE HARLOW & SALLY MORGAN

Kingfisher

KINGFISHER
An imprint of Larousse plc
Elsley House, 24–30 Great Titchfield Street,
London W1P 7AD

First published in 1995 by Kingfisher

10 9 8 7 6 5 4 3 2 1

A CIP catalogue record for this book is
available from the British Library

ISBN 1 85697 381 6 (paperback)
ISBN 1 85697 417 0 (hardback)

Editor: Jilly MacLeod
Designer: Ben White
Art editor: Val Wright
Authors: Rosie Harlow & Sally Morgan
Photo research: Elaine Willis
Cover design: John Jamieson and
    Shaun Barlow
Illustrations: Derek Brazell p. 26-27 (bot.);
    Peter Bull cover; Richard Draper p. 4-5
    (bot.), 6 (right), 23 (top), 29 (bot.),
    30-31; Chris Forsey p.8, 10-11, 12-13
    (bot.), 14 (left), 17 (top), 24; Richard
    Ward p. 5 (top), 6 (left), 7, 9, 12 (left),
    13 (top and bot. right), 14 (top), 15,
    16, 17 (bot.), 18-19, 20-21, 22-23
    (bot.), 25, 28, 29 (top)
Photographs: Ecoscene p. 7, 9 (Morgan),
    20 (Glover), 22 (Cooper), 24
    (Winkley), 25 (Jones); Robert Harding
    Picture Library p.12; NHPA p. 29
    (E. Soder); Panos Pictures p. 10, 14
    (R. Giling); Science Photo Library p. 4
    (G. Garradd), 8 (D. Lovegrove), 17
    (US Dept. of Energy), 19 (H. Morgan),
    23 (M. Bond); ZEFA p. 5, 27 (J. Blanco)

Printed and bound in Spain

About This Book

This book looks at energy and power, and explains how we are damaging our environment by using too much of it. It suggests lots of experiments and things to look out for, as well as ways we can help to make our world a cleaner and safer place.

You should be able to find nearly everything you need for the experiments in and around your home. Be sure to ask an adult to help you when we suggest doing so – some of the experiments could be dangerous to do on your own.

Activity Hints

- Before you begin an experiment, read through the instructions carefully and collect all the things you need.
- When you have finished, clear everything away, especially sharp scissors, and wash your hands.

- Start a special notebook so you can keep a record of what you do in each experiment and the things you find out.

Contents

What is Energy?

Energy is everywhere. We can see it as light, hear it as sound and feel it as heat. There are other forms of energy as well, such as electrical, chemical and movement energy. We use electrical energy for power in our homes, and chemical energy, in the form of fuel, to power our cars. But, as you will see, when we use energy, we often do harm to our environment as well.

Lightning is a giant spark of electricity. The energy from a single flash would be enough to light a town for one year.

factory

bicycles

tanker

house

We use electrical energy to heat and light factories, offices, schools and homes. Electricity is also used to light up our streets at night.

Do it yourself

See how energy can be used to make things turn. You must ask an adult to help you when you light the candle.

1. Draw a snake like the one shown here on a piece of paper. Cut it out and add a red tongue and two eyes. Then tie a length of thread on to the snake's head.

2. Hang your snake above a lighted candle, keeping its tail well away from the flame. Now watch it turn. (Be sure to blow out the candle when you have finished.)

How It Works

When a candle burns, two forms of energy are created – heat and light. The heat causes the air to rise up which in turn makes the snake spin round.

pen

red tongue

scissors

coloured paper

candle

office block

The energy needed to turn the pedals of a bicycle comes from the cyclist. Cars and lorries get their energy from fuels such as petrol and diesel, and some homes are heated using fuel oil. These fuels are delivered in special vehicles called tankers.

lorry

Food for Energy

People use energy to move, keep warm, grow and stay healthy. The energy we need comes from the food we eat.

petrol station

street lighting

cars

Generating Power

Energy can be changed from one form into another. For example, when electricity passes through a light bulb, electrical energy is changed into heat and light energy. Most of the electricity we use today is made in power stations. But power stations need a source of energy too. This usually comes from fuels such as oil, gas and coal. Inside the power station, the chemical energy in the fuel is changed into electrical energy.

cooling tower cools steam

boiler

steam

cables carry electricity

pylon

👁 Eye-Spy

Use the energy in your muscles to light up a bulb by fitting a dynamo light set to your bicycle. When you ride your bicycle, the wheels turn and a tiny generator inside the dynamo makes electricity.

coal supply

steam spins turbine

generator makes electricity

At a power station, coal is burned inside a boiler. The heat turns water into steam, which is used to spin a special wheel called a turbine. This in turn drives a machine called a generator, which changes the movement energy into electrical energy. Power cables, supported by pylons, carry the electricity to homes and factories.

Do it yourself

Make your own steam turbine. You'll need an adult to help you.

1. Cut a circle 8cm across from a thick foil food tray. Pierce a small hole in the centre, then snip in towards the hole with your scissors as shown. Twist the sections slightly to make the blades.

2. Ask an adult to punch two small holes in the top of a full, soft drinks can – one in the centre, the other about 15mm to one side. Empty the drink out and pour about 100ml of water into the can.

Many power stations have cooling towers. The hot steam cools inside the towers and turns back into water. The water is then pumped back to the boiler where it is heated all over again.

3. To make the stand, cut a piece of thick foil 20cm long and 4cm wide. Fold it in half lengthways, then bend it into shape as shown so that it fits across the top of the can. Make a small hole 5cm up on each side of the stand.

4. Fix the stand on to the can with a small screw. Then push a 10cm long cocktail or barbecue stick through the holes in the sides of the stand, threading the wheel in place as you go.

5. Make sure the blades of the wheel are positioned over the small hole in the can. Then ask an adult to put your turbine on a gas cooker over a low heat. As the water starts to boil, the escaping steam will spin the wheel on your turbine.

drinks can

screw

barbecue stick

stand

blades of wheel

heat

7

The Price of Power

When fuels are burned to give energy, they release harmful gases that pollute (poison) our air. Often these gases lie above cities, creating a layer of smog (dirty air). Some of the gases mix with water in the air to form acids. When it rains, the acid in the rain damages forests and lakes. Burning fuel also releases the gas carbon dioxide. This is called a 'greenhouse gas' because it traps the Sun's heat in the atmosphere (the air around the Earth), just like glass traps heat in a greenhouse. The trapped heat makes the atmosphere warm up, which may cause changes in our weather.

Many children suffer from an illness called asthma. They find it hard to breathe and have to use an inhaler. Doctors think that air pollution may be causing the asthma.

Then and Now

carbon dioxide – traps less heat

carbon dioxide – traps more heat

smog

acid rain

fumes

1750

Long ago, there were no factories, electricity or cars. People used horses for transport and burned wood for fuel.

1995

Today, there are many more people. Factories and transport produce tonnes of gases that pollute our atmosphere.

Do it yourself

Try making a smog in a glass jar. You'll need to ask an adult to light the paper for you.

1. Find a large jar and wash it out with water. Don't dry the jar though – you want it to be slightly damp.

A thick layer of smog hangs over New York City, USA, making it difficult to see the buildings clearly.

ice

twist of paper

foil

damp jar

2. Cut a piece of kitchen foil slightly larger than the top of your jar. Put some ice cubes on to the foil.

3. Cut a small piece of newspaper. Fold it a couple of times then twist it up.

4. Ask an adult to light the paper and drop it in the jar. Quickly seal the jar with the foil and ice and watch what happens. (Don't worry if the flame goes out.)

smog

How It Works

The smoke from the burning paper rises up in the warm air. When it reaches the cold air around the ice, it sinks back down to the middle where it mixes with the water in the air to form a smog. When the weather is damp and warm, the same happens over cities that produce a lot of smoke and pollution.

9

The Car Crisis

The car is our most popular form of transport. Every day, across the world, more than 100,000 new cars appear on the roads. But every time we use a car we add more pollution to the atmosphere. This pollution is particularly bad in cities where rush hour traffic fills the streets. It is caused by the cars' exhaust fumes which are made up of harmful gases such as sulphur dioxide, carbon monoxide and nitrogen oxides. They also contain tiny bits of soot. To cut down on air pollution we must design cars that are cleaner to run, and use our cars less often.

Rush hour traffic in Bangkok, Thailand, produces so much pollution that a dirty layer of smog hangs over the city.

How Can We Help?

- Walk or use a bicycle on short journeys.
- Use public transport instead of a car as much as possible.
- On regular journeys, see if your family can pair up with another family and use one car instead of two.

This is how transport might look in the future, with electric cars and buses that cause less pollution, good public transport to encourage us to leave our cars at home, and lots of bicycles.

Catalytic Converters

harmful gases in

cleaner gases out

All new cars have a catalytic converter. This is a device that is fitted into the exhaust system to filter out harmful gases in the exhaust fumes. These cars can only use lead-free petrol and are generally less polluting.

Do it yourself

Ask an adult to help you do this test to see how dirty car exhaust fumes are.

1. Take a square of fine cotton (an old handkerchief will do) and wrap it over the end of a cold exhaust pipe. Hold it in place with a strong elastic band.

2. Ask an adult to turn the engine on for two minutes. Stand well away from the car because the exhaust fumes are poisonous.

3. After the engine is turned off, ask the adult to remove the cotton. Now see how dirty it is.

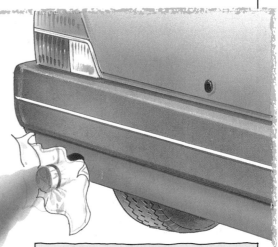

How It Works

The dirt on the cotton is soot, which normally goes into the air. When we breathe in, we take this soot, together with car fumes, into our lungs.

Nature's Fuels

All living things depend on the Sun for energy. Plants use light energy to make their own food – a form of chemical energy. Animals eat plants so they can use the chemical energy stored inside. The fuels we all depend on – coal, gas and oil – also contain a store of chemical energy. They are called 'fossil' fuels because their energy comes from organisms (plants and animals) that lived millions of years ago. When the organisms died their bodies became buried and their remains slowly turned into coal, gas and oil.

Oil Underground

Oil is the fossil remains of tiny animals that died millions of years ago. Oil rigs drill down below the ground or sea bed and remove the oil.

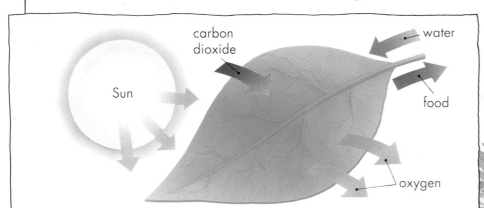

carbon dioxide

water

Sun

food

oxygen

Energy from the Sun

Plants capture light energy from the Sun and use it to make food in a process called photosynthesis. Inside the leaves, the gas carbon dioxide is combined with water to make sugars and a substance called starch. The gas oxygen is produced and released back into the air.

Do it yourself

Do this simple experiment to see whether or not plants need light to grow.

1. Put some damp cotton wool on three glass jar lids and sprinkle a few cress seeds on top.

2. Put one lid on a sunny windowsill, another in a dark cupboard. Cut a small hole in a cardboard box and put the third lid inside. Close up the box.

3. Leave the seeds to grow for a week, keeping the cotton wool damp with a little water.

How It Works

The seeds on the windowsill grow well because they have enough light. Those in the cupboard shrivel and die because, without light, they cannot make food and grow. The seeds in the box grow towards the hole to get as much light as possible.

Coal is the remains of plants that lived in swamps millions of years ago. As the plants died, they sunk layer upon layer beneath the water. The weight of the top layers squashed the bottom layer which eventually became much harder, forming coal.

coal seam

👁 Eye-Spy

Next time you eat bread, cereal, potatoes, pasta or rice, think about where the food has come from. All these foods contain starch made by plants from the Sun's energy.

13

Other Natural Fuels

Coal, oil and gas are not the only fuels that nature gives us. In some parts of the world, such as Ireland and Siberia, people still use a substance called peat. Peat is the first stage in the long coal-making process. It is softer than coal and not as rich in energy, but it can be burned for fuel, and is sometimes used in power stations to generate electricity. Wood also makes a good fuel – many people still use it to heat their homes and for cooking.

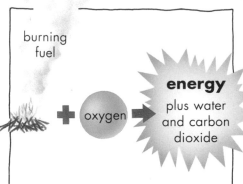

burning fuel + oxygen → **energy** plus water and carbon dioxide

How Fuels Burn

As we have seen, fuels contain a store of chemical energy. When fuels burn they react with oxygen in the air and release heat and light energy, plus water and carbon dioxide. The proper word to describe something burning in air is combustion.

Wood is an important fuel in poor countries where it is collected and burned on fires and stoves for cooking food and boiling water.

Digging for Fuel

Peat is still an important fuel in Ireland, where it is dug up from the ground as small brick-like pieces. The peat bricks are then dried before being burned on fires and stoves in the home.

Low on Fuels

Unfortunately, there is only a limited amount of fossil fuels in the world. Once the supplies have run out they cannot be replaced. This is why fossil fuels are called non-renewable fuels. Wood is also being used up too quickly. Trees can be replanted but they still take over 50 years to grow. So we need to find alternative sources of energy if we are not to run out of power.

oil

coal

gas

How Much Is Left?

There may be enough coal to last for another 300 years. But oil and gas may run out within the next 50 years.

Do it yourself

Make some paper logs to burn as fuel.

1. Tear some newspaper into strips and put them in a large bowl of hot water. Mash the paper into a pulp with a wooden spoon.

2. Scoop up the pulp using a sieve. Pick up a handful of pulp and squeeze out all the water, forming a log shape as you do so.

3. Make several more logs, then leave them to dry out. Then ask an adult to help you make a fire with them.

How Can We Help?

If we all use less energy then the supply of fossil fuels will last longer. Try to turn off unwanted lights, use the car less often, and wear an extra sweater instead of turning the heating up.

newspaper strips

squeeze the water out

paper logs

15

Splitting Atoms

Instead of using fossil fuels to make electricity, we can use 'nuclear power'. The energy for nuclear power comes from a metal called uranium. Like all matter, uranium is made up of tiny particles called atoms. When a uranium atom is split into smaller particles a vast amount of heat energy is released. This can be used to generate electricity. But waste products from nuclearpower stations are very dangerous and are difficult to get rid of safely.

Radioactive Waste

Nuclear power produces a dangerous form of energy called radioactivity. This can contaminate (infect) people and animals, making them very sick. Radioactive waste from power stations is marked with this warning symbol.

Energy from Atoms

neutron fired at atom

atom splits

heat energy produced

neutrons released

Sun's surface

In a nuclear reaction, tiny particles called neutrons are fired at uranium atoms at very high speeds. They split the uranium atoms, causing them to release more neutrons and lots of heat energy. The neutrons bump into more uranium atoms, causing them to split. This is called a fission reaction. Another type of nuclear reaction, called nuclear fusion, is taking place on the Sun's surface all the time.

If there has been a leak at a nuclear power station, scientists use a machine called a Geiger counter to test for radioactivity in the ground and in animals. Sometimes farmers paint their sheep yellow to show they have been contaminated with radioactivity.

The reactor core in a nuclear power station is surrounded by water. The water is heated by the nuclear reaction.

Making Electricity

In a nuclear power station, the uranium is placed in rods inside a 'reactor core'. It is carefully shielded so that the radioactivity cannot escape. The heat from the nuclear reaction heats the water surrounding the core. This hot water is then used to turn water in the heat exchanger into steam. The steam is used to spin the turbines, and electricity is generated.

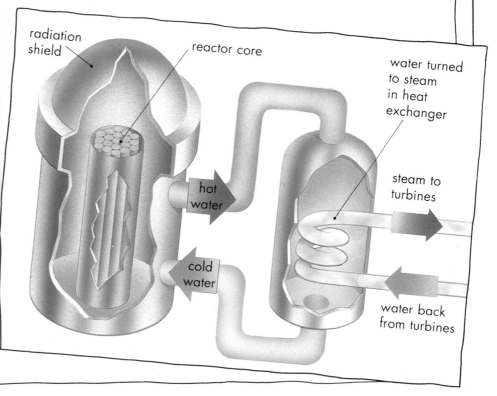

radiation shield

reactor core

water turned to steam in heat exchanger

hot water

steam to turbines

cold water

water back from turbines

Energy from the Sun

The Sun is like a huge power station releasing vast amounts of heat and light energy. It supplies a free source of energy that will not run out. Scientists have devised many new ways of making use of solar energy. Solar panels absorb heat from the Sun, and heat water for homes and factories. Other panels, called photovoltaics, can change light directly into electricity. Both of these ways of using solar energy produce very little pollution.

👁 Eye-Spy

On a hot sunny day, a garden hose pipe acts like a solar panel. It absorbs the Sun's energy and the water inside heats up. Look out for a cat lying on a hose pipe, enjoying the heat.

Do it yourself

Make some tea using energy from the Sun.

1. Take two clear glass bottles the same size. Paint one of them black. Put two tea bags in each bottle and fill them up with cold water.

2. Put the bottles on a sunny windowsill for at least six hours. If you have a thermometer, test the temperature of the water every two hours to see which bottle heats up quickest. Watch the water turn brown as your tea brews.

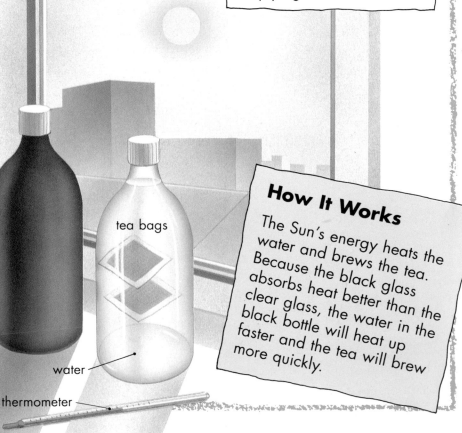

tea bags

water

thermometer

How It Works

The Sun's energy heats the water and brews the tea. Because the black glass absorbs heat better than the clear glass, the water in the black bottle will heat up faster and the tea will brew more quickly.

Trapping the Sun's Energy

Simple solar panels like the one in the diagram are placed on the roof of a house and used to heat water. The water absorbs heat as it circulates through the pipes in the panel, and becomes much hotter.

On a much larger scale, this solar power station in California does the same thing. Thousands of mirrors reflect the sunlight on to tubes containing a special oil. The oil is heated to 575°C and is used to make steam which, in turn, spins a turbine to make electricity.

glass

cold water in

black material to absorb heat

hot water out

water pipes

Called the Sunraycer, this strange-looking car is powered by solar energy. It won the first international solar-powered car race in 1987, travelling more than 3,140km across Australia.

👁 Eye-Spy

Look out for small items powered by solar energy, such as calculators, watches and radios. They use photovoltaic cells to convert the light energy into electricity.

Wind Power

The wind is another free source of energy that can be trapped and used to make electricity. People have made use of wind power for hundreds of years. Windmills were once built to turn a large millstone that was used to grind wheat into flour. Small wind-powered pumps are still used to pump water from wells. About 25 years ago, the first modern wind generators appeared in the USA. Since then, many more have been built all around the world. Because the wind will never stop blowing, wind power is an important source of renewable energy.

Windmills

Traditional windmills for grinding wheat are still found in countries such as Holland. This windmill has four large sails to catch the wind.

Wind Farms

A collection of wind generators is called a wind farm. This one is in California, USA, on the mountains behind the city of Los Angeles. It is very windy here, so the area is ideal for wind power.

On a wind farm, each generator has two or three long narrow blades. As the blades turn in the wind, they turn a turbine which generates electricity.

Do it yourself

Make this wind-powered winch and see how you can use the power of the wind to lift objects into the air.

1. Tape a cotton reel on its side to the top of a length of wood about 25cm long.

2. Cut four pieces of card measuring 5cm x 3cm for your blades. Tape each blade on to the end of a cocktail stick as shown. Then stick the other end of the cocktail sticks into a cork and twist the blades so that they face each other.

3. Stick the cork on to the sharp end of a pencil. Thread the pencil through the cotton reel on the wooden stand. Make sure the pencil turns freely in the hole.

4. Jam a slightly smaller cotton reel (complete with thread) on to the blunt end of the pencil. If the hole is too big, bind the end of the pencil with paper to give a tight fit.

Eye-Spy

An anemometer turns in the wind and is used to measure the wind's speed. See if you can spot one.

materials

smaller cotton reel

larger cotton reel

blade

pencil

cork

cocktail stick

cotton thread

tape

clay weight

wooden stand

5. Unravel about 20cm of thread from the smaller cotton reeel and tie a blob of modelling clay on the end to act as a weight.

6. Blow on the blades to see if your winch can lift the weight. You may need to alter the direction of the blades, or make the weight slightly smaller, to get your machine to work properly. Now try your machine outside in the wind.

21

The Power of Water

Moving water is an important source of free energy. Hundreds of years ago people built watermills by rivers and used them to grind wheat into flour, just like a windmill. Today, moving water can be used to generate electricity. Huge dams, called hydroelectric dams, are built across rivers to generate electricity for nearby cities. The waters of the ocean are also moving, and waves and tides are now being used as a source of energy.

Hydroelectric dams are built across rivers where there is a steep fall in height. The water falling from the top of the dam turns a huge turbine to make electricity.

Do it yourself

Try making your own waterwheel out of a plastic drinks bottle. You may need to ask an adult to help you if you find some of the cutting too difficult.

1. Cut a plastic drinks bottle into three pieces as shown. The middle section should be 8cm deep. Now cut four strips, 2cm wide, out of the middle piece. Cut each strip in half to give eight blades.

plastic drinks bottle

middle section

base section

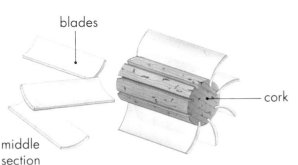

blades

cork

2. Draw eight lines evenly spaced down the side of a cork. Cut slits down the lines with a blunt knife and push a blade into each slit.

This is a tidal barrage, designed to trap the power of the tides. It is built across the mouth of a river, near the sea. As the tide moves up or down the river, the water passes over a turbine, causing it to turn and generate electricity.

turbine

Wave generators (above) are built on the coast. The waves are funnelled up a special ramp, forcing air through the turbines to make electricity.

thread wrapped round cork

tap

water turns wheel

barbecue stick

water

clay

3. Cut away a section of the bottle base as shown. Then pierce two holes just below the rim, one on either side.

4. Cut a wooden barbecue stick in half. Feed each half through a hole and push the sticks into the ends of the cork.

5. Put a second cork on the end of one of the sticks. Tie a length of thread round it and attach a blob of modelling clay. Now put your water-wheel under a tap. Slowly turn the tap on and watch your machine lift the weight.

Energy Underground

Hot rocks beneath the Earth's surface have been used as a free source of heat for hundreds of years. Water moving through cracks in the rocks is heated, often to temperatures of up to 350°C. The hot water can be brought to the surface and used to make electricity. This form of energy is called geothermal energy. It is a very important source of energy in countries such as Iceland and New Zealand.

Sometimes the water and steam heated by the hot rocks burst out of the ground to form geysers and hot springs. In Iceland, everyone heats their homes with water from hot springs.

Hot Rock Power

Geothermal power stations are built in places where there is very hot water in the rocks just below the ground. A pipe is drilled into the rocks to allow steam to escape to the surface where it is used to drive a turbine and generate electricity for local homes and factories. The waste water is pumped back down into the ground to replace the hot water that has been removed.

hot water up

cold water down

hot rocks

The Wonders of Waste

Rubbish could be a cheap source of energy, if only we made more use of it. We have been burying our rubbish in holes called landfills for many years. As the waste breaks down it releases a gas called methane. This is often left to escape into the air, but it can be collected and burned to make hot water and electricity for local homes. Or, instead of burying our rubbish, we could use it as fuel to make electricity.

In some parts of the world, such as India, animal dung is collected and dried. Then it can be burned on fires for cooking and heating.

Do it yourself

Show that rotting waste gives off a gas.

1. Soak some dried peas or beans in water overnight. Then put them in a clear plastic bag.

2. Squash all the air out of the bag and seal it. Then place the bag somewhere warm and leave it for a week. Now see what has happened. (Throw the bag away without opening it once you have finished the experiment.)

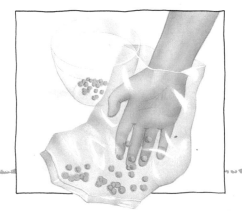

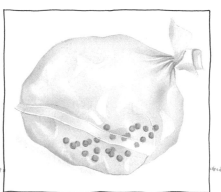

How It Works

The peas or beans soon start to rot as they are broken down by tiny organisms in the air called bacteria. As they rot they give off the gas methane which causes the bag to blow up.

Energy in the Home

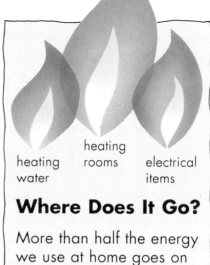

Every home uses energy, but what is it needed for? Modern homes are wired so that electricity can be carried to each room, providing power for lights and items such as televisions and kettles. Fuels such as oil, gas and coal may also be burned in boilers to provide hot water for central heating and for washing. Some equipment is battery-powered. Batteries are stores of energy which contain chemicals that react together to form an electric current. Some batteries can be recharged many times using a power source such as the Sun or electricity.

heating water

heating rooms

electrical items

Where Does It Go?

More than half the energy we use at home goes on heating rooms. A quarter is used to power electrical items and a fifth is used to heat water for washing.

The modern bedroom is very energy-hungry! We use batteries to power toys, and run televisions and radios on electricity.

👁 Eye-Spy

Kitchens use up a lot of energy. Can you work out why? To help you, count the number of electrical items in your kitchen. How many are there compared with your bedroom?

Do it yourself

Do an energy survey in your home to see how much energy you use.

Write down the gas and electricity meter readings. Then go back three hours later to see by how much they have gone up. Take readings at different times of the day and year to see how the amount of energy you use varies.

Heating and lighting also use up energy. But we only need them when it is cold or dark outside.

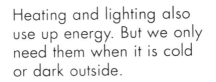

Many people now have computers at home that may be left on for many hours at a time. Computers use up a lot of electricity.

Battery Power

Batteries are a very useful source of energy because they do not have to be wired to the electricity supply. They can be used anywhere to power portable items such as personal stereos. But they do not last very long because the chemicals that power them soon run out.

Save It!

We all use too much energy. If we reduce the amount we use each day we will create less pollution and our fossil fuels will last longer. There are many ways of saving energy in the home. Houses can be built with better 'insulation' to stop heat escaping through the walls and roof. Low-energy light bulbs are widely available, and many electrical goods now carry labels telling us how much energy they use so we can buy the most efficient.

👁 Eye-Spy

Does your family use low-energy light bulbs? They last about eight times as long as ordinary light bulbs and use about a quarter of the electricity.

Do it yourself

Insulation is used to stop heat escaping. Do this simple experiment to see which materials hold heat the longest.

Wrap four bottles in different materials as shown and pour an equal amount of hot water (from the hot tap) into each one. Take the temperature of the water in each bottle, then take it again after 5 minutes, 10 minutes and 20 minutes. Which material gives the best insulation? Which would you wear to keep warm?

newspaper

woollen sock

silver foil

thermometer

plastic bag

Do it yourself

Lots of houses lose heat through draughts. See how draughty your home is with this draught tester.

Cut a square of cling film about 14cm x 20cm and tape it to a pencil. Now hold your tester in front of gaps around windows and doors and see if the film is blown about in a draught.

pencil

tape

cling film

14cm

How Can We Help?

- Make sure our homes are well insulated so heat, and therefore energy, is not wasted.
- Fill up cracks around windows and doors to stop heat being lost through draughts.
- Wear an extra sweater if we are cold instead of turning up the central heating.
- Always use low-energy light bulbs.
- Turn lights off when they are not needed.
- Buy electrical goods that use as little energy as possible.

This home is very energy efficient – that is, little energy is wasted. Its grass roof acts as insulation, keeping the heat in, whereas the small pool helps to keep the house cool in summer.

pool

Tomorrow's Home

The home of the future may look very different from the ones we live in today. There will be many energy-saving features as well as ways of making use of free energy sources, such as the Sun. The sunny side of the house will have large windows and maybe a conservatory to trap heat energy. There will be solar panels on the roof to trap sunlight, and water pipes underground will pick up heat from the soil.

This house has been designed to use energy as efficiently as possible and to make the most use of free energy sources.

House of the Future

1. The north side of the house gets little warmth from the Sun so the windows are small to cut down heat loss.

2. Large south-facing windows and the conservatory allow lots of sunlight in, but the heat cannot escape so the rooms become warmer.

3. All the windows are double- or even triple-glazed (three layers thick) to keep the heat in.

4. Thick insulation in the loft and outer walls stops heat from escaping.

This house in Switzerland has special solar tiles to replace the normal roof tiles. If we use solar power more widely (even in cloudy areas) there will be less need to build new power stations.

Electric cars may be more common in the future. Solar energy could be used to make electricity to recharge the car.

5. Solar panels on the roof trap heat energy and use it to provide the house with plenty of hot water.

6. A heat exchanger pumps water through underground pipes. In the winter, it is used to absorb heat from the soil to warm the house, and in summer it loses heat to the soil to keep the house cool.

7. A heat collector in the ground absorbs heat from the soil which is used to warm the conservatory.

8. The garage is fitted with a car recharger so the car's battery can be recharged overnight.

Index

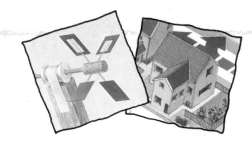
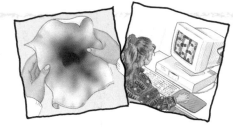

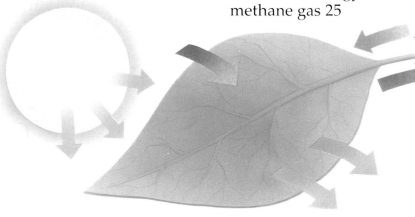